21st Century Skills **INNOVATION** *Library*

Animation

by Trudi Strain Trueit

Published in the United States of America by Cherry Lake Publishing
Ann Arbor, Michigan
www.cherrylakepublishing.com

Content Adviser: Ron Fleischer, Film and Video Department, Columbia College Chicago

Design: The Design Lab

Photo Credits: Cover and page 3, ©AP Photo/Rich Pedroncelli; pages 5 and 15, ©Pictorial Press Ltd/Alamy; page 6, ©Lee Morris, used under license from Shutterstock, Inc.; page 9, ©iStockphoto.com/imagestock; page 11, ©AP Photo/Bookstaver; page 12, ©Mark Bassett/Alamy; pages 17 and 18, ©Photos 12/Alamy; page 20, ©AP Photo/Disney Enterprises, Inc. and Pixar Animation Studios; page 21, ©Andre Jenny/Alamy; page 22, ©22DigiTal/Alamy; pages 25 and 27, ©AP Photo; page 28, ©AP Photo/Marco Ugarte; page 32, Bill Trueit

Library of Congress Cataloging-in-Publication Data
Trueit, Trudi Strain.
 Animation / by Trudi Strain Trueit.
   p. cm.–(Innovation in entertainment)
 Includes index.
 ISBN-13: 978-1-60279-219-7
 ISBN-10: 1-60279-219-4
 1. Animated films–Juvenile literature. I. Title. II. Series.
 NC1765.T74 2009
 791.43'34–dc22   2008002026

*Cherry Lake Publishing would like to acknowledge the work of
The Partnership for 21st Century Skills.
Please visit www.21stcenturyskills.org for more information.*

CONTENTS

INNOVATION IN ENTERTAINMENT

CHAPTER ONE

Animation Fascination

Why do we love **animation**?

Could it be the silly characters? Amazing artwork? Clever stories? Movies, television, and the Internet use animation to entertain, inform, and even sell things. Animation may seem so realistic that we forget we're watching moving pictures. After all, that's basically what animation is: a series of recorded images using film or computer technology. When played back, the images create the illusion of motion.

Flip books and special toys also create animated images. Two-dimensional, or 2-D, animation involves drawings or photographs. Three-dimensional, or 3-D, animation involves objects that have depth. It uses special techniques to create animation of three-dimensional objects. Three-dimensional animation can also refer to

Tom and Jerry is just one example of animation that entertains audiences of every age. Tom and Jerry was created by William Hanna and Joseph Barbera in 1940.

a kind of animation created using high-tech computer equipment. Animation can bring to life almost anything your mind can imagine.

In 1825, an English doctor named John A. Paris developed an optical toy called a **thaumatrope**. It was a round card with an image of a bird on one side and a cage on the other. Two strings were attached to the edges of the disk. By twirling the strings, the disk would spin. The spinning disk made the bird appear to be inside the

Early animators used a sketchpad for their creations. Today, most artists work on computers.

cage! Paris created his device as a way to demonstrate that the brain holds on to an image for a split second after it has moved. Similarly, when we see a stream of still images, our brain connects them. We believe we are seeing movement.

French filmmaker Georges Méliès pioneered **stop-motion animation** in the early 1900s. In stop-motion, you start filming and then stop the camera to adjust, add, or remove items. You then film again and stop once more to adjust, add, or remove items. The process repeats itself until you have filmed an entire action. These were called trick films, because objects seemed to appear and disappear by magic.

Britain's J. Stuart Blackton was a performer who made

Learning & Innovation Skills

By 1877, Charles-Émile Reynaud of France had refined a way to make pictures move. He came up with a device called the **praxinoscope**. Here's how an advanced model of the device worked: drawings on a clear strip were placed inside a hollow drum. As the drum was cranked, a lantern, mirrors, and lens projected the images onto a screen. Reynaud's device was partly based on the technology of another invention called the zoetrope—but he improved upon the idea. He developed a way to project images so that theater audiences could see them. Reynaud also came up with the film **spool** and **sprocket** holes that move film along—inventions we still use today!

With the praxinoscope, Reynaud took a concept that already existed and adapted it. By doing so, he made a useful contribution to the development of animation. Can you think of creative ways to improve objects that you use everyday?

high-speed drawings during his show for American audiences. In 1906, he created an early **cartoon**. In *Humorous Phases of Funny Faces*, Blackton drew faces on a chalkboard that moved, winked, and even grew hair!

Making an animated film is slow work. How slow? Film runs at 24 frames per second. That means it takes 24 still images to make a single second of film!

Many early animators were cartoonists who longed to see their drawings come to life. Winsor McCay was a well-known newspaper comic strip artist and performer in New York. He wanted to create an animated character with a personality and a story. He succeeded in 1914 with *Gertie the Dinosaur*. McCay drew 10,000 images on rice paper to make his seven-minute cartoon. (He even came up with a stage show in which he did tricks with his dinosaur—Gertie was on screen, of course.) McCay's film was an important moment in animation's development and a preview of what was to come.

CHAPTER TWO

The Cartoon Craze

Imagine drawing a character and background thousands of times for only a few minutes of film! Early animators wondered if there was a better way. Two American newspaper cartoonists discovered one at about the same time. Around 1915, an idea occurred to both John Bray and Earl Hurd: why not draw images on **celluloid**? Celluloid is a material similar to plastic.

Using celluloid film was a breakthrough in animation.

It could be made into clear sheets called cels. The idea was to draw characters on the cels and lay them over a pre-drawn background. Using cels over backgrounds that had already been drawn was an important development because it saved time and effort.

Max Fleischer was an animator who worked with Bray. He was searching for a way to make his characters more realistic. Fleischer and his brothers developed the **rotoscope**. It projected single frames of live-action film onto a drawing table. An artist could then trace the images onto paper. The movement of a character became much more lifelike.

In the early 1920s, the popularity of animation soared thanks to the *Felix the Cat* cartoons. They were created by Otto Messmer and Pat Sullivan. Felix didn't talk—at least not yet. It wasn't until the late 1920s that "talkies," or live-action films with sound, became the newest craze. Animators started adding sound to their films, too. It was an exciting idea, even if the **audio** rarely matched up to the action on-screen.

One animator set out to make a film in which the sound did match the animation. His name was Walt Disney. The result was *Steamboat Willie* in 1928. It made Disney a household name and Mickey Mouse a star.

Color film came along in the early 1920s. At first, animators were limited to a few colors. But a decade

Otto Messmer shows off a drawing of Felix the Cat in his studio office.

later, the Technicolor process gave them a rainbow of shades to choose from. Color enhanced the viewing experience. Walt Disney was always on the cutting edge of technology. In 1932, he released *Flowers and Trees*.

It was the first cartoon made in Technicolor. In 1937, Disney released *Snow White and the Seven Dwarfs*. It was the first American full-length animated feature film.

Mickey Mouse started out as a sketch by Walt Disney.

Early stop-motion animation was developed by toymakers and puppeteers in Eastern Europe. In the 1940s, a Hungarian animator named George Pal moved to the United States with his Puppetoons. Puppetoons were animated short features that used wooden puppets. Instead of moving one wooden puppet during shooting, Pal used a separate puppet for each frame. This made the action flow smoothly. The technique was called substitution, or replacement animation. Pal often used thousands of figures to make a Puppetoon that was only a few minutes long!

The 1930s and 1940s saw an explosion of cel animation studios in the United States. Each studio had its own cast of characters. Disney had Mickey Mouse, Donald Duck, Pluto, and Goofy. Warner Brothers had *Looney Tunes,* featuring Bugs Bunny, Daffy Duck, and Porky Pig. Fleischer Studios created Betty Boop and Popeye.

The arrival of television in the 1940s brought animation into the home. In the 1960s, the team of William Hanna and Joseph Barbera produced a string of hit series. These include *The Flintstones*, *Yogi Bear*, and *The Jetsons*. The Hanna-Barbera studio used limited animation. That meant there were fewer drawings per second. The drawings were simpler in form and color, too. The technique made it easier and faster to produce animation. This was a good thing because there was a

21st Century Content

 Animation truly is a global art form. Cartoons and animated features have entertained both children and adults in almost every country. The great thing is that different cultures often reflect different styles of animation. In 1963, Osamu Tezuka created Japan's first animated TV series. It was called *Tetsuwan Atom* (*Astro Boy* in English). Tezuka gave his characters big heads and large eyes so they could better express their emotions. Japanese anime has taken the world by storm with series such as *Speed Racer* and *Pokémon*.

In what ways is anime different from other styles of animation?

growing demand for cartoons. The arrival of the Xerox copier sped up the process even more. It allowed animators to copy drawings onto cels by machine.

By the 1970s, animation was an established part of American life. There were Saturday morning cartoons, prime-time series, holiday specials, and full-length feature movies. Animation had reached its peak. Or had it?

CHAPTER THREE

Welcome to the Digital Age

In the 1980s, the arrival of one particular innovation changed animation forever. It was the computer. Computers allow animators to create characters and drop in backgrounds using computer graphics tools. This type of animation is known as **computer-generated imagery (CGI)**.

In the 1990s, Disney hired Pixar Studios to produce the first computer-animated feature film. The result was 1995's *Toy Story*. The film used

Toy Story, released in 1995, was the first computer-animated film.

Learning & Innovation Skills

 In 1981, the Japanese video game maker Nintendo came out with *Donkey Kong*. It was created by Shigeru Miyamoto. Today, computer animation helps designers create amazing video game effects. But at the time, the technology available to programmers wasn't nearly as advanced as it is now. Miyamoto had a hard time making his character's hair move. To solve that problem, he put a cap on his head. Miyamoto also gave him a colorful outfit to improve his visibility on screen. Miyamoto's hero was originally named Jumpman. That name was soon changed to Mario. *Donkey Kong* became a hit!

Miyamoto was able to find creative solutions to the problems he faced. He went on to design other popular games such as *Super Mario Brothers* and *The Legend of Zelda*. And Mario is still as popular as ever.

computer effects to bring toys to life. How did they do it? An artist made a clay sculpture of each character. Then a computer model was created. Using special equipment and software, an animator then brought the characters to life. Computers allowed artists to create movement and add lighting, shadows, and textures to finish the effect. *Toy Story* was a revolution in animation.

Computer animation is a huge step forward in the industry. It allows animators to create effects that would be difficult or impossible to do the old-fashioned way. Artists can create extremely detailed images and make things such as glass or plastic look very realistic.

By the time Pixar released *Monsters, Inc.* in 2001, animators had mastered digital effects. They could even make the fur on the characters look real. The success

Advances in technology have allowed animators to create detailed characters with realistic movements, such as Sulley and Mike from *Monsters, Inc.*

of movies such as *Finding Nemo*, *The Incredibles*, and the *Shrek* series proves computer animation is here to stay.

For years, people have been interested in the idea of combining animation and live action. An American actor and dancer named Gene Kelly shared the screen with Jerry Mouse in 1945's *Anchors Aweigh*. Animators worked for months to match Jerry's movements to

Audiences were amazed by the innovative combination of animation and live action in *Who Framed Roger Rabbit?*

Kelly's. It wasn't the first time a person and animated character appeared on film together. But it was the first time that live action and animation were combined in such a detailed, skillful way. In the 1980s, the success of the mega-hit *Who Framed Roger Rabbit?* showed that modern moviegoers loved when humans and cartoons got together.

In the 1990s and into the 21st century, CGI allowed filmmakers to blend live action and animation like never before. Animators reenacted a realistic sinking of the doomed ocean liner in *Titanic.* They created armies of soldiers for *The Lord of the Rings* series. They brought museum exhibits to life in *Night at the Museum.* Was there anything animation couldn't do?

In the 2004 animated film *The Polar Express*, actor Tom Hanks did more than lend his voice to the movie. He acted in it, too. Animators used techniques called high-tech motion capture and performance capture. Hanks and the other actors dressed in stretchy bodysuits covered in computer sensors. Sensors were also placed on their faces. As they acted out their parts, their movements were recorded digitally using computers. This data was used to help create each of the animated characters. This method produced some of the most lifelike characters yet. Performance capture allowed Hanks to play multiple characters in the movie.

As computer technology improves, animation becomes more and more realistic. Still, a big part of animation's charm has always been how it explores fantasy and the imagination. It takes us to places we could never go in real life. Maybe that is why both children and adults love animation.

In 2008, *Ratatouille* won the Academy Award for Best Animated Feature. Animated films have had their own Academy Award since 2001.

CHAPTER FOUR

The Draw of Animation

Tony the Tiger has been saying his famous line, "They're g-r-r-reat!" for Kellogg's since 1952.

a company is trying to sell. Advertisers have realized this almost since the first television ads hit the airwaves.

One of the first animated **mascots** was designed by Otto Messmer, creator of Felix the Cat. In the 1940s, he worked on ads for Botany Mills, a textile company. The spots featured a friendly animated lamb that advertised wool ties for the company. Early animated ads were pricey, because they had to be filmed. Back then, TV commercials were usually done live. But animated commercials were worth the extra cost. They helped people quickly identify and remember a product.

Mr. Peanut has been an American advertisement icon since 1918. Today, he is featured in his own computer-animated TV commercials.

Companies discovered that animation could be a powerful tool. They used animated characters to sell everything from shampoo to soda pop. Some of the most popular mascots of all time include Planter's Mr. Peanut, Mr. Clean, and the Pillsbury Doughboy.

In the late 1950s, the makers of Maypo had a problem. The maple-flavored hot cereal wasn't selling well. John Hubley was a former Disney animator and creator of Mr. Magoo. He was hired to design new animated TV ads for the product. Hubley came up with Marky Maypo. The character was inspired by Hubley's own four-year-old son, Mark. In each commercial, the character shouted, "I want my Maypo!" Soon kids around the country were shouting for their Maypo, too. Sales of the hot cereal jumped nearly 80 percent!

21st Century Content

In the 1980s, the California Raisin Advisory Board hired a San Francisco ad agency to help boost the image of its wrinkly fruit. Advertisers Seth Werner and Dexter Fedor were struggling to come up with a snappy idea when they joked about singing raisins. But they were on to something. Their vision was brought to life through Claymation. Claymation is a type of animation that uses images of clay figures. The ads featured singing and dancing raisins. Raisin sales increased by 20 percent!

Companies pay big bucks to advertising firms. They're taking economic and financial risks. No one knows for sure if people will respond to a commercial until after it is released. But the rewards are often worth the risk. A great commercial can mean huge sales of a company's product.

More breakfast cereal manufacturers realized the power of animated advertising. Over the years, millions of kids have become familiar with characters such as Tony the Tiger and the Trix rabbit.

Today, businesses in the United States spend billions of dollars on advertising. Animated characters remain one of the most effective ways to reach consumers, especially kids. Many advertisers rely on popular characters from TV and movies. These include icons such as Shrek and Bart Simpson. Other companies create their own special characters, such as the Keebler Elves.

Animation in one form or another has woven itself into our daily lives. We e-mail electronic greeting cards. We play the latest video games. And, of course, we watch cartoons. The Cartoon Network brings animated programming into 90 million homes in the United States and 160 countries worldwide. Animation is a part of who we are. It has changed a lot over time. And it is still changing as more innovators with new ideas come along. After all these years, animation still has the power to thrill us, to touch us, and to leave us wanting more.

CHAPTER FIVE

Making Their Mark

Over the years, many original and adventurous animators have influenced the art form. Here is just a handful of innovators whose talents have helped shape animation history.

Walt Disney

Walt Disney wasn't a good student. But he was a good artist. As a young man, he

Walt Disney's animated features made him one of Hollywood's biggest stars. Disney went on to create a huge business in film and theme parks.

worked as a commercial artist. He made drawings for catalogs and print ads. But his passion was cartooning. In 1923, Walt and his brother, Roy, created the Disney Brothers Studio. The name was eventually changed to Walt Disney Studios. Together, Walt Disney and his top animator, Ub Iwerks, created Mickey Mouse. Disney originally planned to name him Mortimer. But his wife, Lillian, preferred Mickey. The rest is history. Disney pioneered the use of sound and color in animation. He left a legacy of film classics. These include *Snow White and the Seven Dwarfs*, *Lady and the Tramp*, and *The Jungle Book*—his last film before he died. After Disney's death, the company went on to produce huge hits such as *Beauty and the Beast*, *The Lion King*, and *Toy Story*. The company remains a powerhouse in animation.

Mel Blanc

The way an animated character speaks is just as important as how it looks. And nobody did voices better, or more often, than Mel Blanc. In 1937, Blanc was hired by Warner Brothers to voice the character of Porky Pig. The previous voice artist couldn't get the stutter down. Blanc did it perfectly. If you've ever watched a *Looney Tunes* cartoon, you've heard Blanc. He was the voice of Bugs Bunny, Daffy Duck, Tweety Bird, Sylvester, Pepe Le Pew, Yosemite Sam, Tasmanian Devil, Road Runner,

Mel Blanc provided the voice for Bugs Bunny and other *Looney Tunes* characters for more than 50 years.

and countless others. He also provided the voices for Barney Rubble and Dino in *The Flintstones*. Blanc did almost 400 voices in more than 3,000 cartoons!

Nick Park poses with his characters Wallace (left) and Gromit in 2005.

Nick Park

At the age of 13, Nick Park was making animated movies in his attic in England. In 1985, Park joined Aardman Studios. He went to work finishing a project he started in film school. The film was called *A Grand Day Out*. Park used clay to make the film's stars: a man named Wallace and his faithful dog, Gromit. Park's attention to detail and clever storytelling took stop-motion animation to new heights. His chase scenes were amazing. Park and the Aardman team also produced the movie *Chicken Run* and the *Creature Comforts* series. Park's Wallace and Gromit in *The Curse of the Were-Rabbit* took home the 2006 Oscar for Best Animated Feature Film.

Life & Career Skills

Lotte Reiniger of Germany was a gifted artist. At a time when women weren't considered important to the animation industry, she proved female animators had plenty to say. In 1926, she made *The Adventures of Prince Achmed*. Many consider it to be the world's first feature-length animated film. She lit her stunning silhouettes from behind to create the 300,000 frames needed!

Silhouette animation requires a lot of patience. Artists must be able to deal with time restrictions while still producing quality work. Reiniger was a genius with cutting tools. Her films reflect her lifelong commitment to mastering her craft. It took more than two years of careful, precise work to complete the film. Few have been able to duplicate her graceful, intricate images. In her career, she made more than 60 animated films. The skill and expertise in her works continue to inspire many artists.

Glossary

animation (an-uh-MAY-shin) a series of still images that appear to be moving when shown quickly one after another

anime (A-nih-may) a style of animation that originated in Japan featuring stark graphics and characters with big eyes and expressive faces

audio (AW-dee-oh) television or motion picture sound, or the sending, receiving, or reproduction of sound

cartoon (kar-TOON) a film that is made from a series of drawings or other graphics and that looks to be in motion because of small changes in each frame

celluloid (SEL-yuh-loid) a material similar to plastic that was made into clear sheets for use in animation

computer-generated imagery (kuhm-PYOO-tur-JEN-uh-ray-tid IM-uhj-ree) a type of animation that uses computer technology

mascots (MASS-kotss) characters, people, animals, or objects that symbolize or represent a group

praxinoscope (praks-EYE-nuh-scohp) an early animation device that projected a strip of pictures onto a theater screen

rotoscope (ROH-toh-scohp) a device that projected frames from live-action film onto a drawing table

silhouettes (sill-oo-ETS) dark outlines seen against a lighter background

spool (SPOOL) a reel on which film is wound

sprocket (SPROK–it) a wheel with a rim that has toothlike points that fit into the holes in something to move it through a machine such as a movie projector

stop-motion animation (STOP-MOH-shuhn an-uh-MAY-shin) a type of animation in which objects are adjusted and then filmed or photographed; when the images are quickly played back, the objects appear to move

thaumatrope (THAW-muh-trohp) a toy consisting of a disk with a string that, when spun, created an optical illusion

For More Information

BOOKS

Cohen, Judith Love. *You Can Be a Woman Animator*. Marina del Rey, CA: Cascade Pass, 2004.

Marcovitz, Hal. *Computer Animation*. Detroit, MI: Lucent Books, 2008.

Spilsbury, Richard. *Cartoons and Animation*. Chicago: Heinemann Library, 2007.

WEB SITES

Disney
disney.go.com
Find out more about the innovative creator who paved the way for modern animation

DreamWorks
www.dreamworksanimation.com
Learn more about the animation process and explore behind-the-scenes images

Pixar Studios
www.pixar.com
Visit this site for fun facts about the company's animated films

Index

About the Author

In the sixth grade, Trudi Strain Trueit wrote and directed her first animated film, *Tang*. It was about an alien living on the moon. Now a freelance journalist and writer, she has published more than 40 fiction and nonfiction children's books, including the Innovation Library title *Video Gaming*. Trudi has a bachelor's degree in broadcast journalism. She lives near Seattle, Washington, and enjoys photography, drawing, and going to see animated movies (who doesn't?). Among her favorites are *A Bug's Life* and *The Cat Came Back*.